Envenomators

DEADLY VENOMOUS MAMMALS!

by Joyce Markovics

Consultant: Professor Bryan Grieg Fry
Head of Venom Evolution Laboratory
School of Biological Sciences
University of Queensland, Australia

BEARPORT PUBLISHING

New York, New York

Publisher: Kenn Goin
Senior Editor: Joyce Tavolacci
Creative Director: Spencer Brinker
Photo Researcher: Thomas Persano

Library of Congress Cataloging-in-Publication Data

Names: Markovics, Joyce L., author.
Title: Deadly venomous mammals! / by Joyce Markovics.
Description: New York, New York : Bearport Publishing, [2019] |
   Series: Envenomators | Includes bibliographical references
   and index.
Identifiers: LCCN 2018014139 (print) | LCCN 2018017000 (ebook) |
   ISBN 9781684027064 (ebook) | ISBN 9781684026609 (library)
Subjects: LCSH: Poisonous animals—Juvenile literature. |
   Mammals—Venom—Juvenile literature.
Classification: LCC QL100 (ebook) | LCC QL100 .M36 2019 (print) |
   DDC 591.6/5—dc23
LC record available at https://lccn.loc.gov/2018014139

For more information, write to Bearport Publishing Company, Inc., 45 West 21st Street, Suite 3B, New York, New York 10010. Printed in the United States of America.

10 9 8 7 6 5 4 3 2 1

Contents

Cute but Deadly

It was nighttime on April 8, 2012. Wildlife **biologist** George Madani was **trekking** through a thick rain forest in Borneo. Out of the corner of his eye, he spotted a small, furry animal in a mango tree. He had seen this strange, big-eyed creature before. It was a slow loris—one of the world's few **mammals** that produce **venom**.

Wildlife biologist George Madani

A slow loris is a small, slow-moving **primate**. It lives in southern Asia and is active mostly at night.

Gunung Mulu National Park

Borneo

Arctic Ocean

Asia

Europe

North America

Pacific Ocean

Africa

Atlantic Ocean

Indian Ocean

Australia

South America

Antarctica

Southern Ocean

Borneo is a large island in southern Asia. George was in Borneo's Gunung Mulu National Park when he discovered the slow loris.

George climbed the mango tree to get a closer look. As he got higher, the slow loris became frightened. It tried to back away and tumbled out of the tree. George quickly leapt to the ground to return the small animal to the tree. The slow loris, afraid for its life, lifted its arms above its head and bared its teeth. Then, as George gently grabbed it, the animal sank its sharp teeth into his middle finger.

George was bitten by a Kayan slow loris (shown here).

George's finger after the slow loris bit him

Fighting to Survive

"It was a very painful bite and the loris was **reluctant** to let go," remembers George. Within two minutes of being bitten, George started to feel tingly all over his body. Then, he felt as if his jaw, ear, and foot were being stabbed with tiny pins. "My face was already swelling considerably," said George. He knew he needed help—and fast.

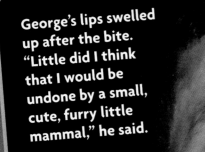

George's lips swelled up after the bite. "Little did I think that I would be undone by a small, cute, furry little mammal," he said.

George raced to a **health clinic** at the edge of the forest. By then, he felt sick to his stomach, had chest pain, and struggled to breathe. He was worried he might die. George finally arrived at the clinic, where he was given lifesaving medicine. "If I hadn't been so close to readily available medical aid, I don't know what would have happened," said George. He continued, "If I can't serve as a good example, then I can certainly serve as a warning. Leave the loris alone!"

The Mulu National Park Health Clinic in Borneo, where George was treated

A slow loris's venom is stored in **glands** near its elbows. When it feels threatened, it raises it arms above its head and sucks the poison from the glands. Then, the animal mixes the poison with its **saliva** before it bites.

7

World's Strangest

The slow loris is one of a handful of known venomous mammals. Another is the duck-billed platypus—one of the world's strangest mammals. It has a bill, webbed feet, and lays eggs, like a duck. Yet the platypus has a beaver-like tail and a long, furry body like an otter's.

Platypuses are found only in Australia. They live mostly in the water, where they hunt for worms, shellfish, and insects.

What makes platypuses even more unusual is their **toxic** weapon. Male platypuses have bony stingers on their hind legs called ankle spurs. The spurs connect to special glands that contain powerful venom. While not deadly to humans, the venom causes pain that's so **severe**, the strongest painkillers can't treat it. Australian Keith Payne learned about the effects of platypus venom firsthand.

A male platypus's ankle spur

Platypus venom is strong enough to **paralyze** or kill small animals.

Spurred by a Platypus

In May 1991, Keith Payne was on a fishing trip in Queensland, Australia. He was surprised to see a platypus sitting on a log beside a stream. When he walked towards the animal, it didn't move. *How odd*, he thought. Fearing the animal was sick or hurt, Keith tried to pick it up and put it back in the water. As he did, the platypus tightly curled its body around Keith's arm.

Platypuses rarely attack people. They will do so only if they feel **threatened**.

Then, the platypus drove one of its large ankle spurs into the top of Keith's hand. It drove the one on its other leg into Keith's middle finger. "There was immediate severe pain," Keith remembers. The pain was so horrible, in fact, Keith compared it to **shrapnel** wounds he got when he was a soldier. As the pain shot through his arm like a hot knife, his hand swelled to double its normal size.

Keith Payne (above) used to be a soldier in the Australian Army.

A Painful Plight

Unfortunately, Keith was nowhere near a hospital. He ran to his car and began a four-hour drive to find a doctor. As he drove, the pain and swelling worsened. Keith worried that he wouldn't get help in time. Finally, he found a doctor, who gave him a very strong pain-relieving drug called morphine. However, it had little effect. The doctor sent Keith to a nearby hospital for more treatment.

A road in Northern Queensland like the one on which Keith drove

A female and male platypus

Scientists believe that male platypuses use their spurs to fight over females. If a male stabs another male, the loser becomes temporarily paralyzed.

At the hospital, doctors gave Keith a drug that blocked all feeling to his hand. Finally, after six **grueling** hours, the **agony** was over. However, 48 hours later, Keith still had pain, swelling, and couldn't move his hand. Six days later, Keith had only 25 percent movement in his fingers. More than ten years after he was spurred by the platypus, Keith still experiences some pain and stiffness in his hand.

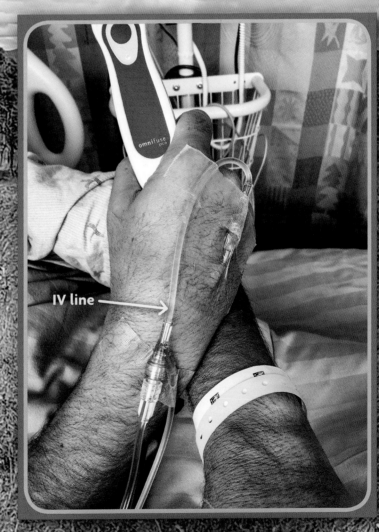

IV line

Keith received medication through an IV line like the one shown here.

Shrew Spit

While platypuses stab their victims with ankle spurs, some shrews attack with venomous saliva. Shrews are small, mouselike animals with beady eyes and pointy **snouts**. Two **species** in particular, the North American short-tailed shrew and the water shrew, are venomous. The venom comes from glands located in the shrews' lower jaw.

The water shrew spends much of its time looking for food in ponds and streams.

The short-tailed shrew has been known to hunt birds twice its size.

A shrew's bite is not deadly to humans, but it can cause a bad rash, swelling, and pain.

Shrews' venom contains a neurotoxin—a poison that specifically targets **nerve cells**. The tiny animals use their toxic saliva to stun and paralyze insects and other small animals. The shrews then store their food alive—sometimes for as long as 15 days—until they're ready to gobble it up!

A shrew makes a meal out of a large grasshopper.

Solenodons

The **rarest** of all venomous mammals is the solenodon (so-LEEN-oh-don). Solenodons live on two small islands in the Caribbean Sea. They **inhabit** thick forests and are active only at night. These creatures look like large shrews, with sharp nails and long, flexible snouts. "They've got tiny little eyes and they don't have particularly good vision," says scientist Jose Nunez-Mino.

Solenodons are about the size of a rabbit. They have a musky smell—like a goat or a wet dog!

A solenodon's venom can cause extreme pain and swelling—much like a rattlesnake's venom.

Like shrews, solenodons have glands in their lower jaw that produce venom. They have needlelike teeth with grooves, along which the venom flows. Solenodons hunt insects, snails, and small frogs under the cover of night. "They use their long noses to probe the earth," says Jose. However, because people rarely encounter them, little else is known about these odd animals.

A solenodon's needlelike teeth

Jose Nunez-Mino carefully handling a solenodon

Poisonous Spines

Unlike shrews and solenodons, hedgehogs don't make venom—but they're experts at using it! These small mammals have short legs and prickly spines covering their bodies. They rely on their spines to defend themselves against attacks from foxes, dogs, and other **predators**. However, they can also turn their spines into toxic spears.

Spines

Hedgehogs live mostly in western and northern Europe.

Hedgehogs are known to kill poisonous toads to **harvest** the toads' poison. The hedgehogs bite toxic glands on the toads' bodies and then mix the poison with their saliva, creating a foamy fluid. Finally, the little mammals smear the toxic mixture on their spines. When an enemy attacks, it gets a mouthful of spines—tipped with toad poison!

Hedgehogs lick their spines to cover them with poison. This is called "self-annointing."

Poison oozing out of a toad's skin

Much to Learn

Because venomous mammals are so unusual, scientists want to learn more about them. Scientists are especially interested in studying their venom and its many **properties**. They're also looking into whether some of the toxins in the venom might be useful to people. John M. Stewart, a **biochemist**, has found that a **peptide** in northern short-tailed shrew venom could be used to help treat migraine headaches and prevent wrinkles.

A scientist holding a shrew

The venom of the slow loris is also being studied. Scientist Anna Nekaris started The Little Fireface Project to research these venomous primates. Beyond studying their venom, she and fellow scientist George Madani are on a mission to educate people about these special little animals. Anna and George hope to show people that the slow loris is a complex creature in need of protecting—and not just a cute face.

Slow lorises do not make good pets—especially because of their venomous bite!

Scientist Anna Nekaris

Slow lorises are among the most **endangered** primates in the world. The forests where they live are being cut down at a fast rate. Also, because they are so cute, many are collected **illegally** as pets.

Venomous Mammals
— PROFILES —

	Kayan Slow Loris	Solenodon	Water Shrew

DESCRIPTION	Kayan slow lorises have round heads, big eyes, and small ears. They have fluffy fur and strong hands and feet, which they use to climb trees. They live in forests in Borneo.	Solenodons are only found on two Caribbean islands. They look like large rats with long, flexible snouts and scaly tails. Their fur is coarse and can vary in color from tan to brownish black. They have long claws to dig under soil for food.	Water shrews live throughout Europe and in parts of Asia. They have long snouts and small eyes and ears. They have short, black fur and white bellies. They hunt for food in water, and their fur traps pockets of air to help them swim.
LENGTH	Up to 10 inches (25 cm)	Up to 15 inches (38 cm)	Up to 4 inches (10 cm)
VENOM and Its Effects	The loris's venom can cause itchy red skin, low blood pressure, muscle aches, breathing difficulties, and heart problems.	The solenodon's venom can cause breathing difficulties, paralysis, and spasms.	The water shrew's venom can cause itchy red skin, pain, and swelling.

Glossary

agony (AG-uh-nee) extreme physical or mental suffering

biochemist (bye-oh-KEM-ist) an expert in the chemistry of living matter

biologist (bye-OL-uh-jist) an expert who studies living things

endangered (en-DAYN-jurd) in danger of dying out

glands (GLANDZ) body parts that release chemicals

grueling (GROO-ling) very tiring

harvest (HAR-vist) to gather or collect

health clinic (HELTH KLIN-ik) a place where patients are given medical treatment or advice

illegally (il-LEE-guh-lee) in a way that is not allowed by law

inhabit (in-HAB-it) to live in

mammals (MAM-uhlz) warm-blooded animals that have fur or hair and drink their mothers' milk

nerve cells (NURV SELZ) special cells in the body that make up the nervous system

paralyze (PA-ruh-lize) to make someone or something unable to move

peptide (PEP-tide) a chemical made of substances called amino acids

predators (PRED-uh-turz) animals that hunt others for food

primate (PRYE-mate) an animal with hands, feet, and forward-facing eyes

properties (PROP-er-tees) qualities or characteristics

rarest (RAIR-ist) least common

reluctant (ri-LUHK-tuhnt) not willing

saliva (suh-LYE-vuh) a watery liquid in the mouth; it helps with chewing, swallowing, and digestion

severe (suh-VEER) very bad or intense; extreme

shrapnel (SHRAP-nuhl) small pieces of an object that exploded

snouts (SNOUTS) the nose and mouth parts of animals

species (SPEE-sheez) a group of similar animals that can reproduce

threatened (THRET-uhnd) in danger of being harmed or attacked

toxic (TOK-sik) harmful or poisonous

trekking (TREK-ing) making a long, hard journey

venom (VEN-uhm) a toxic substance made by some animals

Index

Bibliography

Grant, Tom. *Platypus (Australian Natural History Series).* Clayton, Australia: CSIRO (2007).

Wilcox, Christie. *Venomous: How Earth's Deadliest Creatures Mastered Biochemistry.* New York: Scientific American (2016).

Read More

Blake, Kevin. *Deadly Scorpion Sting! (Envenomators).* New York: Bearport (2019).

Caper, William. *Platypus: A Century-long Mystery (Uncommon Animals).* New York: Bearport (2009).

Goldish, Meish. *Deadly Lizard Bite! (Envenomators).* New York: Bearport (2019).

Learn More Online

To learn more about deadly mammals, visit
www.bearportpublishing.com/Envenomators

About the Author

Joyce Markovics has written over 100 books for young readers. She would like to dedicate this book to Michelle—and all of her other young friends at Claremont School in Ossining, New York.